AF480004

Two Days Before Dying

Lessons Learned

By M. E. Teller

Copyright © 2023 M. E. Teller

Dedication

I dedicate this book to all Friends and Families everywhere in the hope they have the conversations suggested by the epilogue contained at the end of this story.

About The Author

The Author is a true story teller, writing for over 15 years, narrating the stories of true-life situations. Having a background in International Auditing provided a writing skillset that has led to a second career in documenting true situations to be enjoyed by the reading public. Currently, compiling a set of short stories of the true lives of people who are living and those who have passed. The Author enjoys writing and research and spare time hobbies of game night and event planning.

Introduction

It was the spring of '97, a cold and snowy March 4th. She was dying, and she was 80 years old. At 6 am, she passed. Her daughter, the youngest of 5 children, was by her side. There were funeral arrangements to be made and people to contact; no time for grieving now, tears, yes, but grieving, no; maybe later.

Yes, later. About three weeks later, her daughter, Elizabeth, became severely ill and was admitted to the same hospital her mother had passed away in three weeks earlier and just three rooms away.

Elizabeth appeared to be dying herself. The doctors were stumped. They tried every test to discover her illness and provide a cure; all tests came back negative.

Two days before she would have died, the illness was diagnosed, and Elizabeth was started on a 3-week program to cure her.

In the spring of '05, again Elizabeth was back in the hospital. Different hospital, different circumstances. This time, Elizabeth's blood count dropped to 4. The doctors could not explain how she was still alive. Two more days, and she would have been dead.

Why was this scenario repeated after eight years?

She received three units of A+ blood, she was tested for every test the doctors could think of to no avail, and she was released.

One question remains: why did this course or journey take place a second time? Was something not learned the first time?

Sometimes, no matter how hard you try, you get placed in a situation for reasons you have no control over. There is a "why," obviously, but it needs to be discovered and addressed, otherwise, it will be repeated again.

The purpose of this writing, I believe, is the reason.

This needed to be written and, of course, read. This is why each time, two days before dying, Elizabeth was saved?

Contents

Chapter One
Beginnings

Elizabeth's mother was born on October 13th, 1916, and yes, it was a Friday. She grew up on the streets of New York, and her mother worked in a Laundry. She had a hard life, not many extravagances. Elizabeth did not know much about her mother's life before she was born 35 years later.

Elizabeth was the youngest of 5 children, and being the youngest, probably the closest, living with her the longest.

However, there was never any time to talk about things like, "How did you meet dad?", "How did he propose?" "Were you engaged long?" "Do you still have your wedding dress?"

Elizabeth's mother taught her a lot, like how to make the best apple pie, the best meatballs and spaghetti gravy. She taught her how to clean the house, do the shopping and the laundry, and make fresh pasta.

She also taught her how to act like a lady and how to curtsey.

She helped her with her homework, quizzing her on her multiplication tables; no calculators in those days, and her mother was the type of person who was true to tradition.

She decorated the house for every holiday, even Presidents' Day. She changed the curtains with the seasons. Every Christmas there was a fresh Christmas Tree, no matter how scrawny, and always presents.

She made Thanksgiving and Christmas special holidays, baking all the traditional cakes and cookies. Just before the holidays, she would take all 5 Children to Robert Hall for new outfits for the holidays.

There were also Birthday Cakes for each Birthday, which she baked from scratch. She was always kidded about having a big box of scratch in the kitchen.

Elizabeth remembers one time when it was raining so hard that her mother came down to the school lunchroom with lunch because she did not want her children walking home for lunch in the pouring rain. She brought tuna sandwiches and hot cocoa. Elizabeth never forgot that!

I know this sounds like a page out of the book-I Remember Mama---but readers needed to know the type of person Elizabeth's mother was.

Elizabeth's mother's name was Julia!?

Chapter Two
Mothers' Life

Julia was a pretty woman. She would remind one of Kate Smith. She never wore makeup except when she went to the annual Christmas Party with her husband at his job. Elizabeth remembers being in her crib when she was four years old when her mother came in to kiss her good night, and she exclaimed, "Mommy, you look just like a movie star."

Julia took very good care of her family; every Saturday Night for dinner, she would make Sirloin Steak and French fries, and on Sunday, home-made pasta and fresh sauce, which was called gravy in those days. For Easter, they all went to Robert Hall's department store to get their Easter Sunday outfits.

They all lived in a simple house in Corona, Queens. By all, I mean nine people: Mother, Father, five children, 1 Grandmother and 1 Aunt, not to mention one dog, two goldfish and two turtles. There was an enclosed porch where you first entered the house, which led into the foyer. To the right of the foyer was the living room; it was a large room where the Christmas tree was displayed each December. Off the living room was a large dining room. It held a large dining table, large enough to seat ten people, 12 at times when a company would come over, which was rare. The dining room also contained Julia's sewing machine, which her mother gave her as a wedding gift. Julia would sew almost all of the family's clothes. She tried her best to teach Elizabeth to sew more than once, but Elizabeth had a mental block against it. She also tried to teach her how to knit and crochet, but again, Elizabeth could not pick it up. This was just not something she enjoyed; however, she did maintain her mother's love of cooking, especially baking. To this day, she still makes the best apple pie. Off the Dining room was a very large eat-in kitchen where all the weekday meals were taken; the dining room was reserved for Saturday and Sunday only. The rule of the house was that no matter what, after dinner, all the dishes must be washed and dried and put away, and the kitchen was then closed. Off the kitchen was the door to the basement, and the hallway which led to the front door and the staircase leading upstairs, where there was one bathroom and three bedrooms, with a door leading to the attic, where there were two more bedrooms.

As you could well imagine, space was tight. Elizabeth's bed was in her parent's bedroom until she was nine years old. This was when her grandmother died and her oldest sister got married. Her second oldest sister moved to the attic, two brothers moved into the second largest bedroom, and Elizabeth finally got a room of her own.

Chapter Three
Life

Elizabeth's life was not easy either; however, it was far different from her mother's. After high school, she went to a school to study Computer Programming, which was suggested by her brother.

This was paid for by money left to her by her grandmother. After six months of training, she got her first job at a law firm in Great Neck, Queens. This lasted six weeks, mostly due to the fact that it was for computers she was not trained in. She held several jobs since this first job, but her career did not start until she went to work for a Major Bank in downtown Manhattan. This Bank had a tuition refund program that paid for her education. She would work full time at the Bank then on to school full time at night, getting home by 9 or 10 pm. What took most people two years to complete took her seven years. During this time, she managed to purchase a small house on Long Island in '77. The house in Queens was sold in '78, and her mother moved in with her.

Elizabeth and her mother lived in this house happily until '89, when her mother fell down a flight of stairs. The cause of this was diagnosed as a TIA or small stroke. After this, life changed.

Elizabeth tried to manage her mother's care at home. However, it became too difficult, so she quit her job in the city and tried to establish a consulting business from her home. This did not work too well, because although she was at home most of the time, she could not bring in enough income to carry the house and expenses. She arranged to get a home health aide to care for her mother so she could make an income.

As the years passed, Elizabeth's mother's condition deteriorated until one of her hospital stays admitted her to a Nursing home. This was determined to be the best for her since she needed more than a health aide could provide. This was a very hard decision for Elizabeth; she knew her mother hated hospitals, but Elizabeth could no longer care for her mother and run a business at the same time.

Chapter Four
The Nursing Home

Julia was admitted to a Nursing Home in Rockville Centre in '92; she was 75 at that time. Elizabeth knew her mother was not happy there, but this was the best for her. At least they had some activities for her, and every once and a while, there was a man who came in and played the accordion. Julia loved music, especially the accordion. Elizabeth recalls when she was a little girl, there was a man in the neighborhood who would play La Vi En Rose on his accordion and she would hear her mother humming the tune. In addition to the music, the home would have a Pet Day, where local residents would bring dogs and cats around to the residents' rooms to visit. Julia loved dogs. Elizabeth recalls two family dogs, Red, an Irish Setter and Weed, a German Shepard. Red was a very rambunctious dog. One time, when Julia was taking her for a walk, Red spotted a squirrel. Red took off, dumping Julia in the trash can and breaking Julia's arm. Nevertheless, Julia still loved her Red.

Elizabeth tried her best to ensure her mother was as comfortable as possible in the Nursing home. She would do her laundry once a week, because the Nursing home would wash the clothes but would not iron them. Elizabeth remembers her mother would always iron the family's clothes, even underwear and sheets. Jula took pride in caring for her family, and Elizabeth always remembered that, so even though it was hard, she always washed and ironed her mother's clothes every week.   Elizabeth would also visit her mother every day, stopping by either before work or after work just to see if everything was ok. Sometimes, she would get out of work late, and when she got there, her mother was already asleep, so she would kiss her mother goodnight, check with the Nurses, and head home.

Elizabeths' home was an extended cape cod house in Valley Stream, too big for Elizabeth to manage on her own, along with work and her mother in the Nursing home; therefore, although she was brought up with the kitchen rule - all dishes done and put away and the kitchen cleaned - sometimes the rule was not always adhered to, not to mention unmade beds from time to time and dust on the furniture; She did the best she could. This went on for the first three years that her mother was in the Nursing home; until then, Elizabeth was just barely managing. The house became too much for Elizabeth to handle, so she decided to sell it and move into an apartment where she would not have to care for the lawn, garden, trash take out and all the repairs that owning a house required. Elizabeth saved as many memories that would fit in a four-room apartment and either sold the rest thru yard sales or threw them out for trash.

When Elizabeth looked through the contents of the house before selling or trashing the items, she came across old birthday cards that were never sent with five- or ten-dollar bills in them. There were over one hundred dollars stashed in the bar, there were gifts still in boxes that she received for Christmas or Birthdays, never used. She also found a Damask tablecloth that was only used on Thanksgiving and

Christmas. China sets like new used only on holidays. One small box, when opened, contained some of her memories now forgotten. There, amid all this paraphernalia, were the crayon-drawn "I Love You Mom" cards from when all her children were small. There were even some old report cards and trinkets made by the children.

In one small moment, after going through all of these memories, Elizabeth sat down and thought with tears in her eyes, is this what life boils down to, all the memories of a single life hitting the curb, because there was nowhere else for them to go! Three-quarters of a century of living and what was left, your children, to deal with it all.?

Chapter Five
Hospital Stays

Julia had been back and forth to the hospital several times during her stay at the Nursing home, and although Elizabeth signed a DNR order, she always managed to get better and return to the Nursing home after each hospital stay. One day, while visiting her mother, Elizabeth spoke frankly to her mother, stating, "I know you don't like hospitals, and I know you don't like being here, yet you struggle so hard to get well and come back, but you don't have to, everything was taken care of so it is ok, you could go with the angels". The next time Julia went to the hospital, it was her last. Elizabeth promised her she would not die alone. She would stay with her until she passed, and she did.

Gone was the weekly laundry chore, gone were the daily visits, gone was the caring. Gone but not forgotten.

There was a lot to do on the day of Julia's passing. All personal effects had to be removed from the Nursing home, Funeral Arrangements had to be made, and people needed to be notified. This was all accomplished with the help of friends and family. The next two days, a wake was held and on the third day, Mass and Burial.

On March 7th, it was all over. A life that was here for eighty years was gone. All that was left were memories - the good times, the bad times, some pictures, remnants of a life, a life that created and touched so many other lives over in the course of eighty years, gone in three days, as fast as we come into this world is as fast as we go out; but where do we go?

Chapter Six
The Conversation

Elizabeth had been sick since before her mother went to the hospital. She was battling stomach issues, but she brushed all this aside to take care of her mother's dying days. Once everything was taken care of, she allowed herself to become deathly ill. She thought it was the flu, so she self-medicated, drank plenty of water, rested and took Tylenol. She kept everyone away for fear of infecting them.

On the fifth day of feeling like this, she noticed blotches on her legs, and she could hardly walk, and she was extremely weak. She gave in and called her doctor; he told her to go to the Emergency Room and he would meet her there. She was too weak to drive, so she asked a friend to drive her there. The doctor saw her there and immediately admitted her.

She remembered seeing her sister-in-law, her friends, her sister and her brother-in-law, then she dropped off to sleep.

She was tested for everything, but they could find nothing. Elizabeth was getting weaker and weaker. They then decided it was Chron's Disease, so they treated her for three weeks. Overall, Elizabeth was in the hospital for over a month. The doctor told her that if they could not solve this situation, she would have been dead in two days.

It was during this hospital stay that Elizabeth's first journey began.

Chapter Seven
Journey 1

Elizabeth's bed was located in a ward where three other patients were residing for various ailments. Elizabeth was in the ward because she had no Health Insurance.

Once Elizabeth began her treatment, she began to notice the other patients around her. Also, because she was in the hospital for such a long time, many of the patients were released and replaced with new patients. Elizabeth met a variety of different people from varied ethnic and religious backgrounds.

Although she recalls many of the situations of the other patients, she could not find any rhyme or reason for her to be placed in this situation, one she had no control over.

As she thought back, she recalled an old movie about five people you meet in heaven, where a maintenance man at a carnival died, and his journey took him to meet a lot of people along the way.

The one patient she remembered most was a frail black woman, her name was Dotty. She was 86 years old and hospitalized for a severe case of colitis. Every day, her daughter would visit her, and on Sundays, the entire family would visit to pray around her bed and then share the Sunday meal. Dotty was the only patient who was still there when Elizabeth was discharged. Elizabeth also recalls Dotty's daughter, Helen, because of all the patients' families who came to visit. She was the only one who spoke to her, offering any kindness or assistance.

Elizabeth's family and friends were there whenever they could, and her best friend and sister called almost every day.

Even though there was a TV to keep her company, a hospital ward is a lonely place, especially when you are used to being as active as she was.

To this day, Elizabeth believes she was deliberately placed in this situation for a reason; she was meant to spend time with this variety of people, but why? Was it to see how people act and treat each other? Was she meant to learn something from this experience? Eight years later, she would learn she did not have the disease she was diagnosed with. So, what was she treated for? Was this sickness the excuse for her to be placed in this situation?

Elizabeth did learn a lot from this experience, more than she realized at the time. Looking back, she can remember how all those people acted and reacted. She recalls that many of the common courtesy's were lost. There were few, if any, "Thank Yous" or "Would you mind if…" or "Can I help you" phrases offered. The nursing staff was so overworked that they could not take 2 minutes to talk to their patients, and when it was time for a shift change, there was not a nurse to be found. Doctors would stop by but for all of 1 minute, and then they were gone; no time for questions and answers.

Looking back on this, one month, Elizabeth wonders where it all went wrong. She thought, what happened to people? Did the pace of life become so fast that people could no longer remember how to treat each other? Was the art of conversation a dying art, or did people no longer have time to practice it, or did they just no longer care?

Chapter Eight
Journey 2

Eight years later, in April '05, almost to the day, Elizabeth found herself in the hospital again and again two days before she would have died. Why? Could it be associated with the number 8? She was born on the 8th day of the year; 8 was always her lucky number, and her middle name contained eight letters - Patricia.

But why, again, in a situation over which she had no control? This time in a semi-private room. Next to her was a woman, a stage 4 diabetic who was in the hospital for two months. The doctors could no longer do anything for her, yet she cursed and yelled at the doctors and nurses hourly.

Then Elizabeth was moved to another room. Next to her, this time, was a woman who reminded her so much of her mother. Every night, her daughter would stop by after work. This reminded her of herself, visiting her mother after work. She recalls the daughter trying to coax her mother into exercising and walking. Talking to her about eating right to keep up her health.

Out of this scenario, Elizabeth saw herself with her mother, Julia, over eight years ago.?

Chapter Nine
Lessons Learned

After Julia had her first stroke, Elizabeth would force her to get out of her favorite chair and go for a walk; sometimes, this erupted into a fighting match because her mother did not want to move; the more Elizabeth yelled, the less her mother wanted to move. It was the same for her eating habits. She took no water and only had milk with her coffee. As for talking, Julia hardly spoke; sometimes, Elizabeth thought she forgot how.

It reached a point where Elizabeth became the mother, and her mother became the daughter; true role reversal.

Elizabeth did the cooking, cleaning and shopping. At times she even had to help her mother with dressing and bathing.

Elizabeth's last, or should I say second hospital stay, flashed this all back to her upon seeing the white-haired woman next to her, interacting with her daughter.

Seeing this made her realize something, which she thought was the meaning behind all of this. Even though there comes a time when daughters become the mothers and mothers become the daughters, daughters should look at their own actions toward their mothers. Let them be; don't force them to do or not do something you want them to do, even if it is for their own good. They won't see it this way.

Talk with them and ask them about their life; this is quality time that neither of you knew about. This winter of their life should not be spent in angry misgivings. Ask them about the family recipes that live in their minds alone, write them down, try them out, and adjust them until they taste just right. Go through the old pictures and find out who these people are. Elizabeth threw out so many photos because she did not know who those people were.

The saddest thing is not knowing what we could have known!?

Chapter Ten
Lessons Passed

Looking back, what was actually seen by Elizabeth was the interaction between family members. The elderly or sick and their younger family members; Elizabeth would not realize this until her second hospital stay. Once she realized this, although too late for her, she knew she needed to get this information to others who were in a situation that she had gone through.

She felt an unrelenting need to spread this information around to those who needed it now. She needed to tell the daughters everywhere who were in a similar situation - "It's ok to finish your parent's sentences for them, help them eat, help them dress, help them walk or push their wheelchairs; and if you should find yourself in a situation where you begin to sound like your parent - scolding a child - STOP, THINK, - they are not children, you can't correct them by yelling at them - it won't work."

Instead, let them be; relax your anger. They may not be with you much longer.

Believe it or not, they know, just as you or as Elizabeth found out, there was no point in arguing, no point in yelling, no point in getting upset. It wouldn't do any good. It wouldn't change anything.

The course was set, and it must be run, no matter what obstacles were in the path.

Elizabeth's experience occurred twice. Once she lived through them and again, she was given a rare opportunity to view it through someone else's experience. She was also given the opportunity to live to talk about it. She believed the reason she did not die, even though she came so close: TWICE!

The reason she did not die was that she had a purpose to fulfill. The purpose of sharing the knowledge she was given was to pass this information along.

Maybe if someone had told her before she was thrown into this situation how to handle it, it would not have been so hard.

Elizabeth and her mother used to joke about death, telling each other whoever died first to send a letter and tell the other what it was like. They also used to joke, saying it must be nice in heaven because no one ever came back, and of course, the old cemetery joke that the reason there was a fence around the cemetery was that people were just dying to get in.

But, you know, the actual details about their final requests were never discussed, almost as if well, if we don't talk about it, it wouldn't happen; wrong, thought Elizabeth. Everyone needs to know. Everyone needs to talk about it. Do you realize how hard it is for those left behind to figure out all the details of how you want to leave this world?

Consider funeral arrangements, what dress you want to be buried in, shoes, eyeglasses, and hairstyle. Do you have any last words you want your family and friends to hear? Do you want to be buried or cremated?

We never know when or how we will leave this world, but all families and friends should have this conversation, and if possible, it should be recorded so it can be known to those left behind.?

Chapter Eleven
The Purpose

It was the fall of '07 now, and Elizabeth was telling her story so that she could fulfill her purpose and hopefully not wind up in any other hospital where she would have to view any more mothers and daughters experiencing her experiences all over again.

It is said that every life tells a story; however, very few write them down and pass them along.

This was a true story. It actually happened; this could be anyone. You could have substituted your name for Elizabeth's, but the message would be the same.

Treat others as you want to be treated, and communicate your feelings and last wishes with your families and friends.

Elizabeth's story has not ended yet, but now, being in the winter of her life, she would make her last words and wishes known to her family and friends.

She is having this book published for them, dedicating it to them so they would have it as a conversation starter to make them and their families aware of the lessons she learned and pass them on to their families and friends.

Elizabeth's saddest thought about life was when all the people who knew you when you were young and active have passed on, and there is no one left here in the world who knew about your life. Did you really exist?

We are all here for a really short time. Our lives are just a drop in the bucket; the average person has no future recognition like Marilyn Monroe, Katherine Hepburn or Lucille Ball.

They will live on forever, but will we??

Epilogue

For all sad words of tongue and pen, the saddest are these—
"It might have been"

John Greenleaf Whitter

This book was not written only to open everyone's eyes but to ultimately act as a conversation starter.

The Author left a series of lined note pages here to record questions and answers of the discussions had with family members. Obviously, the best way is to record these discussions with a recording device, which will not only allow the results of these discussions but also preserve the voices of family members.

The Author's wish is that all readers of this book will get a copy of this book and offer it to extended family members so the legacy will continue.

This book is intended as a keepsake to be handed down the family tree as a legacy for generations to come.?

CONVERSATION STARTER
NOTES/PHOTOS

CONVERSATION STARTER
NOTES/PHOTOS

CONVERSATION STARTER
NOTES/PHOTOS

CONVERSATION STARTER
NOTES/PHOTOS

CONVERSATION STARTER
NOTES/PHOTOS

CONVERSATION STARTER
NOTES/PHOTOS